ROBO-VAC

Susan Gates

Illustrated by Scoular Anderson

OXFORD
UNIVERSITY PRESS

1

The New Robot

Connor's Great-Gran moved into
a new flat.

'It's made for old people. She's got
lots of machines to help her,' said
Connor's mum. 'Even a little robot to
do the cleaning.'

'A robot?' said Connor. 'Cool!'

He rushed round to Great-Gran's to have a look.

Robo-Vac sat on the kitchen floor. It looked like a silver frisbee.

It had wheels and two arms.
One arm was a grabber, for picking
things up. The other arm was a tube,
as soft and grey as a baby elephant's
trunk. That was for vacuuming. It had
a little brush for a tail.

Connor pressed a button.

Robo-Vac started to hum. It waved its arms. Its little tail twirled.

Two blue lights, like eyes, lit up on top of it.

'Aww,' said Connor. 'How cute!'

Then Robo-Vac got busy and started to clean the kitchen.

It picked up a bag.

It vacuumed.

It brushed and polished.

All the time, it sang a happy little song.

But Great-Gran wasn't happy.

'I don't like machines,' she said.

'I'm going to send it back.'

As if it had understood, Robo-Vac stopped cleaning. It sat under a table. Its eyes grew dim. It stopped its happy little song.

'It looks so sad,' said Connor. 'You
can't send it back.'

'*You* have it, then,' said Great-Gran.
'Take it with you.'

'What, me?' said Connor. 'I'm going
to play football!'

But the little robot was already
humming happily after Connor.

2

'Stop That!'

Connor walked to the park. Robo-Vac buzzed along behind him, cleaning the pavement.

'Cool!' said Connor's mates. 'Your own little robot!'

'Stay there!' Connor told Robo-Vac. 'We're going to play football.'

The game started. At first, Robo-Vac kept out of the way.

Then, all of a sudden, Robo-Vac
dashed onto the pitch.

It tripped Jason up and started to
clean the football!

'Stop that!' said Connor.

But every time the ball got dirty,
Robo-Vac dashed out to clean it.

'Can't you stop it?' shouted Connor's mates. But the little robot seemed to have a mind of its own.

'You're spoiling our game,' said Connor. 'You're just a big pest!'

As if it understood, Robo-Vac's eyes grew dim again. It stopped singing. It looked really sad.

Connor couldn't be cross with Robo-Vac. It was only trying to help.

Great-Gran didn't want it. Who would look after it, if he didn't?

'Come on, Robo-Vac,' sighed Connor. 'Let's go home.'

Robo-Vac hummed along behind him, happily vacuuming up the leaves.

3

Robo-Vac Cleans Up

Connor took Robo-Vac up to his bedroom.

It started cleaning the floor.

'Hey!' said Connor. 'I like my bedroom messy!'

But the little robot cleaned up everything – dirty socks, homework and pocket money.

'You are starting to get on my nerves,' grumbled Connor.

He should switch it off. But he couldn't do it.

It was so happy and looked at him with such trusting blue eyes. It couldn't help the way it loved cleaning.

'I'll have to wait until its batteries
run down,' Connor sighed. 'But it's
driving me mad!'

Suddenly, Connor had a brilliant
idea.

He took Robo-Vac to his sister
Gemma's bedroom.

Gemma was as tidy as Connor was messy. Nothing in her bedroom was ever out of place. She would get on with Robo-Vac really well.

'Hey, Gemma,' said Connor. 'Do you want your own cleaning robot?'

17

'Wow!' said Gemma. 'A cleaning robot. What a great idea.'

Connor went back to his own bedroom. At last he'd got rid of Robo-Vac. He threw a few things on the floor. Now he could be as messy as he liked...

4

'Take It Back!'

The next morning, Gemma rushed into Connor's bedroom. Robo-Vac was humming behind her.

'Please take it back!' Gemma begged Connor. 'It's driving me crazy!'

'But you *like* things tidy,' said Connor.

'That's just the point,' Gemma said. 'There was nothing for it to *do* in my bedroom. So it sat in a corner and looked really sad.'

'I know,' sighed Connor.

'So I *untidied* my bedroom,' said Gemma, 'to make it happy again!'

'You didn't!' said Connor. He couldn't believe it. His tidy big sister had messed up her own bedroom, just to make Robo-Vac happy.

'Please, please, please take it back,' Gemma begged. 'I hate being messy.'

'Well, I *hate* being tidy,' said Connor.

21

Connor and Gemma stared at each other. Robo-Vac was already busy, picking up Connor's trainers and putting them neatly in pairs.

'We've got to *do* something about Robo-Vac,' said Connor.

'But what?' said Gemma.

5

Robo-Vac
Finds A Friend

'What's that noise?' said Connor.

BBRRRR... a deep, growling sound
was coming from outside.

'It's Dad, mowing the lawn,' said
Gemma.

BBRRRRR...

Robo-Vac stopped cleaning. It went
very quiet and still.

It seemed to be listening.

Then, suddenly, the little robot
whisked out of the bedroom.

It slid down the
stairs.

'Where's it going?'
asked Connor.

Robo-Vac clattered
out into the garden.
'After it!' said Gemma.

Connor and Gemma ran downstairs.
Robo-Vac was sitting on the lawn.

Its blue eyes were sparkling like
stars.

'What's it staring at?' said Gemma.

Dad pushed the mower past. The
little robot's eyes glowed even brighter.

'It's looking at the mower,' said Connor.

BBBRRRR! The mower roared past again. Robo-Vac's cleaning arms waved about in excitement.

'I think it's in love,' said Gemma.

Connor let out a hoot of laughter. 'In love? Don't be so silly!'

'Don't laugh!' said Gemma. 'You'll
hurt its feelings.'

Connor looked again. Could
Gemma be right?

'If I was Robo-Vac,' said Gemma,
'I might fall in love with that mower.
Look how tidy the grass is, now!'

Dad put the big mower back in the
shed. Robo-Vac went in behind them.
Gemma peeped through the window.

'Awww,' said Gemma. 'Just look at
those two. How sweet!'

Connor peeped in. Robo-Vac sat next to the mower. The little robot was gazing at it with adoring eyes.

'We're free at last!' said Connor. 'Now Robo-Vac's in love, it's not interested in cleaning up after us!'

Connor rushed up to his bedroom and threw a few things around.

In *her* bedroom, Gemma was busy tidying her books into neat rows.

Out in the shed, Robo-Vac was cuddling up to the mower.

'How great,' said Connor, stretching out on his bed. 'Everyone's happy.'

About the author

My son Alex gave me the idea for this story. His bedroom is really messy. But he says, 'Don't tidy it, I know where everything is.' Like Connor in the story, he'd love a pet robot. However, just like Connor, a fussy little neatness freak like Robo-Vac would soon begin to get on his nerves!